CONVICTED

New Hope for Ending America's Crime Crisis

Charles Colson
Daniel Van Ness

CROSSWAY BOOKS • WESTCHESTER, ILLINOIS
A DIVISION OF GOOD NEWS PUBLISHERS

Cover photo: The Image Bank © 1988

First printing, 1989

Printed in the United States of America

Library of Congress Catalog Card Number 88-71801

ISBN 0-89107-506-2

Bible verses are quoted from *Holy Bible: New International Version,* coypright © 1978 by the New York International Bible Society. Used by permission of Zondervan Bible Publishers.

Table of Contents

Acknowledgments

We are grateful for the assistance of gifted and dedicated colleagues in preparing this book. David Carlson provided invaluable aid researching and organizing early drafts of the manuscript; Mike Gerson was a great help as well. Ellen Santilli Vaughn's skilled editorial hand patiently melded our different styles into cogency. Tom Crawford reviewed the manuscript and provided valuable suggestions and additional data.

We are also grateful to the staff and volunteers of Prison Fellowship and Justice Fellowship who faithfully demonstrate the truth of the principles we have outlined in this book. In so doing, they bear witness of the gospel to a world which hungers for good news.

Above all, we are grateful to the Lord, who has invited us all to understand and know Him:

"Let not the wise man boast of his wisdom or the strong man boast of his strength or the rich man boast of his riches, but let him who boasts boast about this:

that he understands and knows me, that I am
the Lord, who exercises kindness, justice and
righteousness on earth, for in these I delight,"
declares the Lord.

(Jeremiah 9:23, 24)

Introduction

From 1969 to 1972 I served as Special Counsel to a President who had run and won on a "law and order" ticket. As a fiercely loyal aide to Richard Nixon, I helped write and shape some of his toughest statements on crime and punishment.

But then something happened I'd never imagined possible. I became a federal prisoner, and I saw the criminal justice system from the inside.

I worked in the prison laundry, running the dryer. Next to me was the former chairman of the board of the American Medical Association. He ran the washing machine. He was a skilled doctor who could have been made to work giving free medical help to the poor, contributing to the community rather than costing it about $15,000 a year to keep him in prison. But there he was, stirring suds.

Don't get me wrong. We deserved punishment for our crimes. But couldn't punishment be designed so it allows nonviolent offenders to pay back society— rather than costing taxpayers huge amounts of money and taking up cells needed to house violent criminals?

And all around me in prison were men lying on

their bunks, staring dully at the ceiling, growing more apathetic and sullen by the day. The system, I saw firsthand, wasn't doing anything to restore or rehabilitate them; it was just warehousing them. It's not hard to understand why 74 percent of released prisoners are rearrested within four years.

Then I got out of prison. And for the past thirteen years I've worked in prisons across this country and around the world. I've spoken with thousands of inmates. I've sat down with those who run the institutions. And I've met with dozens of political leaders in the U.S. and abroad. And from all these different groups I've heard the same message: total frustration with prisons.

The message is clear. Ask prisoners, taxpayers, victims, correctional officials, or politicians who are willing to tell you the truth: they will all answer you that our criminal justice system is not working.

I think it's high time we faced the real facts about the criminal justice crisis in America. We need prisons for dangerous offenders—but nearly half the people who are in prison today are there for nonviolent offenses. According to Department of Justice figures, it costs an average of $80,000 to build a maximum security cell, and an average of $15,900 a year to house a prisoner there.

That's a shocking cost for taxpayers to pay to confine someone convicted of a nonviolent offense.

That offender should be working in community service, paying back those he wronged, learning to contribute as a responsible member of society rather than sitting idly in an expensive prison cell, growing bored and bitter and plotting his next crime.

What we need now is a whole new philosophy, a radical new approach to crime, victims, offenders, and communities. The exciting thing is, that is best achieved when we implement sound Biblical principles in our approach to crime. Look at restitution, the Biblical method for punishing nonviolent offenders. Restitution works. It contributes something useful to the victim and to society. It's redemptive for the offender. And it's far cheaper than prison.

Clearly it's time for some good ideas—some Biblical ideas—to make their way to Washington and state capitals around the country. But change will come about only if citizens like you and me are informed, aroused, and righteously indignant. We've got to demand constructive change; and we've got to demand real answers, not rhetoric, from politicians who pander to public fear to perpetuate themselves in power.

That's why we've written this book. I was a law-and-order conservative in the late sixties and early seventies. I still am. I simply want a system that provides real law and order—as well as justice and righteousness. And the present system is not doing that: our prison population is growing ten times faster than the general population, and yet crime continues to skyrocket.

I asked Dan Van Ness to coauthor this book with me. Dan and I have worked shoulder to shoulder in criminal justice issues for the past eight years. He has become, I believe, one of the leading authorities in America on criminal justice and particularly on the Biblically-based concept of Restorative Justice we'll be outlining in the pages that follow. Dan and I have worked together with citizens' groups and state legislatures: we've seen that reforms actually work.

If you get the idea that I'm angry with the present system, you're absolutely right. I am. And you should be too. The public has been ripped off long enough by political demagoguery and gross inefficiency that seems to punish victims and taxpayers far more than offenders. There is no excuse for the failure and waste that have characterized our criminal justice system in America for far too long.

But if I'm angry, I'm also hopeful. I know that God is sovereign, and when His people are aroused to seek true justice and righteousness in society, constructive change is possible. It's happened before. It was the passion of Christian conscience that fueled the fight against the slave trade and slavery itself, that fought for the safety and rights of factory workers in an era of industrial abuses, that compelled the great fight for civil rights in the sixties, that even today sustains the pro-life, anti-abortion movement.

The time has come for Christians to take up the battle in the criminal justice arena. I pray this book will provide a critical first step. I hope it will help you become informed about the very real problems in America's prisons, jails, courtrooms, and communities—and to see what you can do about them.

Charles W. Colson
Washington, D.C.

One

Victims, Criminals, and Society

Greg Browning yawned and stretched beneath the cool sheets as he woke up that summer Saturday morning. It was clear and sunny outside—a great day to wash the car and then head out to the lake.

Greg slipped on a T-shirt, some shorts and sneakers, and headed downstairs to the kitchen. Joan was at the table, reading the paper and drinking coffee. Greg looked over the headlines: the usual assortment of weather disasters, political upheaval, and crime reports. Such things seemed far away from his peaceful life that morning. He kissed his wife, and went out to the carport.

Except for a lawnmower off in the distance, the neighborhood was quiet. Greg backed the car out into the driveway, then gathered up a bucket, sponge, and hose. He sudsed the car, then rinsed and buffed it to a gleaming shine, his thoughts on the rest of the day ahead.

At first he didn't notice the man walking up the driveway—but suddenly a tall, muscular man in his mid-twenties stood before him. He seemed agitated, waving his arms and shouting at Greg. "I'm going to steal your car," he roared, shaking his finger in Greg's face. "And you know what? You can't do a thing to me!"

Greg's confusion turned to fear as the man shoved him in the chest. The two locked arms, wrestling each other to the driveway. As Greg hit the hard pavement, his arm snapped. He knew it was broken.

Inside the house, Joan heard her husband's scream of pain and rushed to the kitchen window to see the two men struggling in the driveway. She ran to the phone, called the police, and returned to see the stranger jump up and swing into the driver's seat of their car. Greg lay on the ground, moaning. As Joan ran out the kitchen door, the man drove off with a screech of tires.

By the time the police arrived, Joan had helped her husband get up and walk to the kitchen, keeping his fractured arm as still as possible. One of the officers sent out a radio alert with a description of the Brownings' car and Greg's assailant.

Two patrol cars soon spotted the vehicle; as they did, the driver tried to elude them by cutting through the grounds of a local high school. He skidded into a parked car, and was stunned but not hurt as the police pulled him from the Brownings' damaged car.

A peaceful Saturday morning had turned into a nightmare. Greg had been attacked by a stranger, his arm broken, his car stolen and damaged. Unfortunately, this was just the beginning of the Brownings' troubles. Victimized by a criminal, they would now become victims of the system.

The police had assured Greg and Joan that they

would be kept informed of the progress of the case against the young man. But over time the Brownings heard nothing at all from the police or the District Attorney's office. Joan finally called the prosecutor's office to find out the date of the preliminary hearing. She was shocked to hear it had already taken place. She was assured she would be told when the case went to trial.

Weeks later Greg and Joan were finally summoned to appear at a hearing. Although both of them would miss work, it would be worth it to find out what was going on. The day before the hearing, Joan called the court to confirm the time and place. "Weren't you told?" the clerk asked her. "The hearing has been postponed."

The Brownings made an appointment with the District Attorney's office to demand some answers. "Why aren't you telling us what is happening?" they asked in frustration. "When will we be able to have our say?" The person handling the case was blunt: "You need to understand something: this is not your case. You just happen to be the victims. This was an offense against the state, and that's how we handle it."

The authorities saw the whole case as the state's business—not theirs. Joan had never been so angry. "But it was Greg who was assaulted and whose arm was broken!" she sputtered. "We had to pay the medical bills! We had to pay to have the car fixed!" What followed was even more frustrating.

The man who attacked Greg was released, without the Brownings' knowledge. When Joan happened to call again for information about the status of the case, she was shocked to discover that the man was now in the custody of his mother (even though he was twenty-five years old), with the condition that he wouldn't bother the Brownings again. Small comfort to Greg and Joan. To date, the Brownings have no idea whether Greg's attacker was ever convicted, where he is, or if he will ever walk up their driveway again.

Greg Browning was the victim. But the justice system was less concerned about Greg or his suffering than with processing his attacker's case. Joan concludes: "It was a real shock to see the system wasn't working for us, and that it didn't help us in any way. Who's the system there for?"

A fair question.

Forgery was the last thing you'd expect from Tim Starnes. A shy, overweight kid, the youngest of five children, he grew up in a Christian family. Lonely and self-conscious because of his weight, Tim tried to buy friendship from schoolmates with little $5 bags of marijuana. To purchase them, he would sneak into his parents' bedroom, steal his mother's checks, forge and cash them.

Ann Starnes had no idea anyone was forging her checks. At first, she figured she had simply lost them. Then notices began arriving from the bank charging her $30 for every bounced check. She called the police; soon a warrant was issued for the unknown forger. The police tracked Tim down easily.

When Ann found out that it was her son who was responsible, she immediately wanted to drop the charges. But matters had gone too far for that. A warrant had been issued. Now the whole affair was the state's business.

Tim was tried and convicted of forgery and passing bad checks. He had no previous criminal record, had committed no act of violence. But the judge wanted to make an example of him, and sent him to prison.

Terrified by the idea of her young, naive son behind bars and haunted by the fact she had unwittingly turned him in, Ann Starnes had a nervous breakdown. She knew exactly what would happen to Tim. "I knew they would abuse him. He was one day over eighteen years old. He was a pretty boy. I knew what would happen to him in prison." And it did happen.

Tim was raped. He tried to resist the assault, and suffered all the more. His attackers, all older and stronger, beat him with metal pipes. He still bears the scars—physical and emotional—from the attack.

"He was a child," Ann says. "A very gentle child. He made a mistake; he went to prison for it. And prison has hardened him. He's not the sweet kid who went away."

No question about it: Tim Starnes broke the law. But was prison rape a fair punishment for him? Thrown into prison for forging checks, this once-gentle teenager went behind the walls nonviolent and confused. He may well come out violent and bitter; once abused, he may become an abuser himself.

In his case, we can only wait and see.

Brian Smith wears the Grim Reaper tattooed on his arm—an appropriate ornament for someone who has compressed a long career of violent crime into his twenty-four years. All told, Smith has been charged with sixteen crimes in Florida and Kentucky since 1983. His spree started with auto theft, drug possession, and assault. His sentence was five years probation.

Then he was convicted of illegal ownership of a

.357 Magnum revolver, a violation of his probation. He served three months in prison. Later he was charged with battering his girlfriend and fracturing her cheekbone. He served three more months.

In 1986 Brian Smith visited his father in Kentucky. Following an argument between the elder Smith and his girlfriend, the two men beat the woman up, tied her arms and legs, and set fire to her house. Somehow she managed to escape. For his part in the crime, Brian Smith was given five years probation, serving no prison time at all.

In August 1987, Smith's wife called police to complain that her husband was in a rage and was threatening her and her two-year-old son Josh. When police arrived, Smith, swaying and cursing, reeking of alcohol, struck one of the officers. Charged with battery of a law enforcement officer and resisting arrest, he was sentenced to two and a half years in prison.

But Florida's prisons, like many in the country, are crowded far beyond capacity. For every prisoner who goes into the prison system, one must come out. The incoming prisoner is often a drug offender, a burglar, a thief. The one released could be a murderer or armed robber.

So after serving less than one fifth of his sentence—six months—Smith was released from prison on July 14, 1988 in order to relieve overcrowding.

Soon after, the killings began.

On July 26, the body of Richard Simmerman, victim of an armed robbery, was found shot to death on the floor of a Pick Kwik, a convenience store. On August 2, Hal Ramsay was killed in a robbery at the Continental Inn. And on August 7, Charles Muhia, a dishwasher at a Sizzler restaurant, was murdered in a similar holdup.

Brian Smith was arrested by police and charged with three counts of first-degree murder and three counts of armed robbery.

The *St. Petersburg Times* commented:

> Smith, now accused of murdering three store clerks . . . was traded for a newcomer. Smith out of prison; a burglar or a thief in. That's the formula for Florida corrections today. It's a formula for disaster. Because lawmakers have failed to make intelligent choices about which criminals need imprisonment and which criminals can safely and more effectively be punished through alternative sanctions, the prisons operate on a gate valve. One in; one out. . . . So the violent criminal, in many cases, is released to make room for an offender who likely poses no threat to society.

The stories of Greg Browning, Tim Starnes, and Brian Smith are true—and sadly illustrate the human tragedies exacerbated by our crippled criminal justice system. And those stories don't just happen to "other people." Each of us is a potential victim.

Two

America's Criminal Justice Crisis

If you haven't already been a victim of crime, you will be. This is not a warning or a theory. It is a fact.

A 1988 Justice Department study found that 99 percent of Americans will be victims of theft at least once in their life. Eighty-seven percent will have property stolen three or more times. Eighty-three percent will be victims of violent crime at least once. Four in ten will be injured in a robbery or assault.

If the crime against you is serious enough—if you are assaulted, robbed, or raped—you'll be thrust into an impersonal, disorienting, and often hostile system of "justice" that will most likely leave you confused and threatened even further. You'll enter an unfamiliar world of police, hearings, lawyers, and judges that touches your own world only at points of violence and loss.

What you will find there will shock you: inefficiency, low morale, prison overcrowding, revolving door release, indifference at every turn. It's a system on the brink of incoherence. Not even those who run it defend it. It is a joke to criminals, a mystery to victims, a scandal to taxpayers.

The signs of crisis in the American criminal justice system are everywhere.

Prison Overcrowding

In recent years the "get tough on crime" mentality has resulted in enormous prison population growth.

There were 604,824 prisoners in America in mid-1988—83 percent more than in 1980. Prison construction has not kept pace. Federal prisons are as much as 73 percent over capacity, while state prisons operate between 105 to 120 percent of capacity.

As of mid-1988, thirty-seven states were under full or partial court order because of overcrowded, inhumane, unconstitutional prison conditions. One California judge noted that prisoners were being held in less space than state law required kennels to give dogs and cats!

Prison Costs

In this decade of soaring budget deficits, governments are spending enormous sums of money to build and operate prisons. It costs an average of $15,900 to keep an inmate in prison for one year—about the same as sending a student to Harvard University. Because of the overcrowding problem, state and federal governments are rapidly building more and more prisons—to the tune of almost $5 billion in the last fiscal year alone. And when all that money is spent, American prisons will still be over capacity.

A sobering case in point is the California state prison system. By 1990 California will have added thirty thousand new prison beds to its facilities, at a cost of $2 billion. The continuing prison population explosion, however, has forced the California Department of Corrections to ask for an additional $1.5 to $2 billion. It turns out they need 17,500 more beds. Imagine the shock to California taxpayers when they were told that even after adding space for nearly fifty thousand inmates, by 1995 their prison system will still be thirty thousand beds short!

As a result, the tax burden grows heavier. As we write, the cost of operating California's prison system has risen to a staggering $1.3 billion per year—and it's headed up.

The forecast is similarly bleak across the rest of the nation. The National Council on Crime and Delinquency forecasts that prison populations will increase by 50 percent in the next ten years. Are taxpayers and communities ready for what that will mean?

Skyrocketing Crime

One out of every four households in the U.S. is touched by crime each year. More than six million Americans are the victims of violent crime annually. Nearly 75 percent of all inmates released from prison are rearrested within four years of their release. A study by the respected Rand Corporation found that ex-prisoners are actually *more* likely to commit new crimes than similar offenders who were placed on probation. Crime is an epidemic in America—and the current system doesn't seem to have an antidote.

Forgotten Victims

Crime victims suffer emotional trauma, physical injury, and material losses (nationally, more than $13 billion a year). Too often excluded from any meaningful participation in the criminal justice process, they typically receive no payment for their losses and have no say in the plea bargaining, prosecution, or sentencing of those who have victimized them. In most cases, they serve only as witnesses in the state's case.

Any crime wreaks emotional havoc on its victim, and many leave physical and financial wounds as well. Yet victims are forgotten parties in our nation's criminal justice system.

So who benefits from the current system of justice and punishment?

As Greg and Joan Browning discovered, victims certainly do not. They may as well be invisible. Their suffering is deemed irrelevant. Their losses are not repaid.

Nor do nonviolent criminals such as Tim Starnes benefit. They are stuffed into prisons that are little more than overcrowded warehouses. These "graduate schools of crime" take nonviolent offenders and make them live by violence. They take the violent and harden them further. Of course, prisons are essential for violent and dangerous offenders. But let's not kid ourselves. They do not rehabilitate.

Communities don't benefit either. Across our nation we are promised that get-tough sentences and more prisons will make our streets safe. But that has simply not happened. Overflowing with ever-increasing numbers of inmates, prisons can't be built fast enough. And even as we build more prisons, crime rates continue to rise.

It's hard to think of anyone who benefits from our current system of justice and punishment—anyone, that is, except the politicians whose campaigns feed on this crisis, and the architects and builders who construct the walls and bars of our nation's concrete monuments to failure. Candidates promise to get tough, to lock up criminals and throw away the key, and they succeed in gaining some votes. But the evidence indicates that their solutions have been, at best, irrelevant; at worst, a primary cause of the problem itself.

The 1988 presidential campaign was a good example. Pollsters and analysts agree that Willie Horton's prison furlough was one of the keys to George Bush's victory. (Both candidates, it should be noted, exploited the crime issue. Governor Dukakis accused Mr. Bush of supporting indicted "drug dictator" Manual Noriega.) The election rhetoric played on public fears, greatly distorting what can and should be done about crime and punishment.

It's clear that Willie Horton should never have been released on furlough. That was a tragic decision. But it became partisan fodder—and worst of all, it worked. Public fears were exploited, successful furlough programs across the country were imperiled, and no useful purpose was achieved for the criminal justice system.

What is needed is responsible leadership. Decisive action could address this criminal justice crisis. But before we explore potential solutions, we must first clear away some of the myths.

Three

Getting Tough on Crime?

As we've seen, aside from kissing babies and getting re-elected, talking tough on crime is the most popular of political pastimes. But one point is often forgotten in the midst of all the heated rhetoric. A policy is tough only if it actually works. The so-called law-and-order approach of more prisons and longer sentences surely works as a political strategy. But does it work in the real world of victims, offenders, and communities?

The answer, quite simply, is no.

It isn't as if we haven't tried. The nation's prison population has doubled in the last decade. The inmate population is actually increasing at ten times the rate of the general population. Our country imprisons more people per capita than any other nation in the world except the Soviet Union and South Africa. America's pack-em-in prison experiment is unprecedented in history; we spend billions of tax dollars each year on more prisons, more courts, more police. If stiffer sentences stopped crime, we shouldn't have any crime at all.

But we do. In fact, we have one of the highest crime rates in the entire world.

Baffling? At first glance, yes. But the problem is understandable when you take a closer look at it. As we just noted, tough policies are tough only if they work. The "get tough" approach is defended on two grounds: it discourages potential offenders from committing crimes (deterrence), and it gets dangerous offenders off the streets (incapacitation). Both deterrence and incapacitation could be—should be—important weapons in our war on crime. But ironically, "get tough" policies hamper our ability to use those weapons effectively.

Criminologists agree that harsh penalties won't deter criminals who believe they won't get caught. Most offenders today are convinced they won't get caught. And the following evidence, compiled from federal reports, shows they are right.

Only one out of three crimes is reported to the police. Of that one in three, police make an arrest only 20 percent of the time. This means there are only seven arrests for every one hundred crimes.

But the bad news doesn't stop there.

Nearly half of the people arrested have their charges thrown out by the prosecutor. Eighty to 90 percent of the rest are convicted. Of those found guilty, half are put on probation, 25 percent are sent to jail, and 25 percent go to prison.

In other words, *one* person goes to prison and *one* person goes to jail for every one hundred crimes that are committed.

No matter how tough politicians talk about long prison terms, it simply doesn't mean much to a criminal who knows the odds. This is especially true when the rewards of crime are high. A young New Yorker named Nick offers a good example.

Nick had been involved in organized crime since childhood, and then had made a career of dealing drugs. On its face, drug retail seemed an illogical choice in a state which then had a law imposing a mandatory life sentence for convicted narcotics dealers.

But before Nick started selling drugs, he had worked as a rod carrier on the eightieth floor of the World Trade Center. One slip up there, he figured, and he was dead. For his salary of $18 an hour, he risked his life.

Then he found he could make $300,000 a week selling heroin. If he got caught (which he thought was unlikely), it would only mean life imprisonment. The rewards were great, the possibility of capture was small, and Nick decided the choice was easy. The trade-off was worth it.[1]

Of course, most crimes are not premeditated, carefully weighed choices at all. Crime is usually impulsive. By some estimates as many as eight out of ten crimes are committed through a haze of drugs or alcohol. Crimes done under the influence of passion, impulse, or chemicals are undeterrable, since the offender is not likely to pause and soberly reflect on the consequences of his act.

Convincing evidence refutes the notion that harsher prison sentences will deter crime. Over a twenty-year period (from 1955 to 1975), crime actually increased more in fifteen states where prison capacity grew by 56 percent than in fifteen other states where prison capacity increased only 4 percent.

It wasn't any different in earlier times. In eighteenth-century England, for example, government officials set out to get tough on crime by hanging pickpockets. To reinforce their point and intimidate potential offenders, they conducted the executions in public, before large crowds. But there was a problem. The hangings drew droves of pickpockets, who had a field day stealing the wallets of those gathered to watch the executions of pickpockets.

But even though harsh sentences fail to deter, don't they at least incapacitate: ensure that dangerous offenders are kept off the street? Unfortunately, they may do just the opposite.

As we have seen in the Brian Smith case in Florida, longer and harsher sentences can actually mean that serious offenders serve shorter prison terms. This is because most "get tough" bills are so broadly written that they sweep up many offenders who pose little danger to society. These nondangerous offenders then use up scarce prison space, forcing early release of the dangerous.

The federal government reports that just under half (46 percent) of all state prisoners were sent to prison for nonviolent crimes. And 35 percent of all prisoners have *never* been convicted of a violent crime in their lives! In Florida, where half the state's prisoners committed nonviolent property crimes, 85 percent are classified minimum security. One in eight have never even been on probation.

Consider just two examples. A Texan named Harold swindled three people out of a total of $230 over an eight-year period. In Texas, those three offenses qualified him as a "habitual criminal" and resulted in a mandatory life sentence. He spent eleven years in prison before being released on parole.

Sounds tough, doesn't it? But what most Texans didn't realize is that it cost, all told, about $160,000 to keep this man in prison. This seems an excessive public bill for a $230, nonviolent crime. Harold should have been punished, yes—but not in a way that punished the taxpayers of his state as well.

In Missouri, a probationer was recently accused of stealing a $20 automobile seat cover. The charges were dropped—but the judge sentenced the man to sixteen years in prison because he had violated the terms of his probation. Missouri taxpayers could consequently spend $240,000 on a man accused of stealing $20 worth of property.

Some nonviolent offenders may need to be locked

up because they are professional or career criminals. But it makes sense that most nonviolent offenders should be sentenced to punishments other than prison. This would free up prison beds for dangerous offenders who *should* be kept away from society.

In short, prisons are filled with people they failed to deter. Ironic, isn't it? The "get tough" policy on crime fails on the two very counts on which it is defended—deterrence and incapacitation.

What can be done to really deter crime, to once again bring law and order to our streets and communities today?

We've seen evidence of the mess we're in. Before we can solve it, however, we must understand how we got here. For even the most unintelligible of public policies have their origins in philosophies. The problem is, they're often false ones.

Four

The Roots
of Crisis:

Mistaken Views
of Crime and
Criminal Justice

A fundamental reason for our tangled system of justice is the philosophy that crime is primarily an offense against the state. Remember the reasoning given to Greg and Joan Browning: "You just happen to be the victims. This was an offense against the state, and that's how we handle it."

To students of history (and of the Bible), this may come as a surprise. The legal systems that contributed to Western law—Mesopotamian, Hebrew, Greek, Roman, and Anglo-Saxon—viewed crime primarily as an offense against victims, their families, and their communities.

In part to avoid plunging into an endless cycle of vengeance and violence, ancient cultures developed legal customs and codes that relied heavily on restitution to make up for the victims' losses and help restore community peace and order. The Old Testament, for example, called for restitution even in cases of violent crime:

> If men quarrel and one hits the other with a stone or with his fist and he does not die but is confined to bed, the one who struck the blow will not be held responsible if the other gets up and walks around outside with his staff; however, he must pay the injured man for the loss of his time and see that he is completely healed. (Exod. 21:18, 19)

If a man steals an ox or a sheep and slaughters it or sells it, he must pay back five head of cattle for the ox and four sheep for the sheep. (Exod. 22:1)

How, then, did we get to the system we have now?

Laws began to change during the Middle Ages, around the time of William the Conqueror. During this period, kings were struggling with local barons for political power. In an effort to gain control of the courts, William's son, Henry I, announced a law which covered England with "the king's peace."

Anyone who committed a crime violated this peace, thus violating the king. The king insisted that such cases be brought to his courts, which effectively gave him control over all criminal cases. And because criminal punishments now redressed the fictional "injury" to the king, instead of the real injury to the victim, restitution payments to victims gave way to fines to the state.

The king had not only taken the place of victims before the law; he had also taken away their right to be repaid for their losses.

This turned the purpose of punishment upside down. Rather than focusing on victims (who were by now simply bystanders in the whole process), criminal justice now focused on offenders: why did they break the law, and how could they be punished so that they would not do it again?

This focus on the criminal rather than the victim led to the next major development in criminal justice—the use of prisons as a means of punishment.

Before the nineteenth century, prisons had simply held offenders until trial. But in 1790 Philadelphia Quakers convinced city officials to convert the local jail into what they called the "penitentiary," or a place of penitence.

Believing that criminals were the products of a bad moral environment, the Quakers thought that isolating criminals and providing them with a Bible and time to contemplate it would lead to their rehabilitation. Many of the prisoners, placed in solitary confinement for long periods of time, simply went mad instead.

But such failure did not discourage prison advocates. Offenders were defective, and society would cure them one way or another. So they were herded off into institutions where they could be "socialized" under the prevailing theory and returned to society as productive citizens.

Succeeding generations moved from theories of repentance to hard work, then to discipline and training, and eventually to medical and psychological treatment. Disappointing recidivism rates should have shown that none of these was the key to "graduating" law-abiding citizens from their prisons. But it was too late: imprisonment had become the primary form of punishment in the U.S.

Recently, most criminologists and criminal justice practitioners have abandoned the belief that prisons can rehabilitate.

Former Chief Justice Warren Burger summed it up well:

> We have developed systems of correction which do not correct. . . . If anyone is tempted to regard humane prison reform as "coddling criminals" let them visit a prison and talk with the inmates and staff. I have visited some of the best and some of the worst prisons and have never seen any sign of coddling. But I have seen the terrible results of boredom and frustration, of empty hours and of pointless existence.

But the illusion lives on—even flourishes. In the last twenty years we have imprisoned more offenders than ever before.

So the Western approach to justice and punishment first transformed crime into an offense against the state, not the victim, then enthusiastically began to use prisons for all criminals in the vain hope of rehabilitating them.

Let's look at this issue from a different perspective.

How does the Bible define and deal with crime? Perhaps the place to begin is with the concept of *shalom*, commonly translated as "peace." While we generally think of peace as public order, security, absence of conflict—the king's peace—the Hebrews meant something more. *Shalom* meant the existence of right relationships, harmony, wholeness, completeness. It characterized the ideal relationship between individuals, the community, and God. As a result of these right relationships, the community knew security, prosperity, and blessings from God.

Crime destroyed *shalom*. Offenders broke the harmony that was to exist between them and their victims, their community, and God. New and destructive relationships took its place. The Biblical response to crime, then, aimed to restore right relationships—*shalom*—between the affected parties.

Restitution—paying back the victim—was essential to this process. The Hebrew language itself reflected the linkage between restitution and peace: the word for "restitution" was *shillum*, from the same root as *shalom*.

We have seen that the Old Testament law frequently called for restitution. This formed the backdrop of a familiar New Testament story. When the corrupt tax collector Zaccheus repented of his greed and extortion, he promised to repay fourfold anyone he had cheated (Luke 19:1-10).

Zaccheus' restitution did more than financially compensate his victims. It helped restore the *shalom* that had been broken. And in fact, Jesus acknowledged that Zaccheus' promise of restitution had restored him to the community: "This man, too, is a son of Abraham."

Did this mean there was to be no punishment? Not at all. Restitution was understood to be retributive. And *shillem,* another word related to *shalom,* meant "recompense" or "retribution."

Interestingly, two modern sanctions were not used at all in the Old Testament. Prisons were used only as a means of holding defendants until their cases had been decided (Lev. 24:12), not for punishment. Second, offenders did not pay fines to the state; they repaid their victims.

The goal of Biblical justice, then, was *shalom*: restored relationships between offenders, victims, the community, and God. This was done through restitution and vindication.

How does American criminal justice measure up to this standard? As we see it, there should be at least four elements of justice: securing public order, holding offenders accountable, ensuring repayment of victims, and restoration of community peace. All of these are important.

But our nation's system focuses completely on maintaining public order and punishing offenders. It views crime only as an offense against government, not an injury to the victim or community. It does not require that victims be repaid, or that offenders make things right, or that the community take responsibility to see justice done. No wonder crime has become a crisis in America today. And no wonder that peace, justice, order, and compassion are its casualties.

Five

The Roots
of Crisis:

Mistaken View of
Human Nature

At least our criminal justice system is consistent. It is not only wrong in its analysis of the purposes of criminal justice. It also misunderstands human nature and consequently the causes of crime itself.

For centuries sociologists have tried to identify the genesis of criminal behavior in individuals. Some believed that crime is the result of inferior intellect, or that criminals could be recognized by their appearance, or that crime was determined by economic or genetic factors. (All of these theories share the distinction of having been discredited by the subsequent generations.)

The school of thought that crime is caused by poverty, environment, and societal conditions gained wide acceptance in America two centuries ago, and has led to the escalating use of prisons for convicted offenders. In prison, an offender could be retrained, rehabilitated, in a sense reprogrammed from the exterior factors that had led to his crime.

For American criminal justice has heartily embraced one of the predominant secular myths of modern times: human perfectibility. Its proponents would like us to believe, notes social critic Russell Kirk,

> that education, positive legislation, and alteration of environment can produce men like gods; they deny that humanity has a natural proclivity toward violence and sin.

55

As Ramsey Clark, Attorney General under Lyndon Johnson, wrote, "Healthy, rational people will not injure others." Since people are essentially good, social or psychiatric causes must force them into antisocial behavior. The lesson is clear: the fault lies not in ourselves, but in unemployment, racism, poverty, or mental illness. It follows that the solution to crime must lie in addressing those outside factors. Clark, embracing this human engineering view, argued:

> The basic solution for crime is economic—homes, health, education, employment, beauty. If the law is to be enforced—and rights fulfilled for the poor—we must end poverty. Until we do, there will be no equal protection of the laws. To permit conditions that breed antisocial conduct to continue is our greatest crime.

This view has been articulated in the highest levels of government. President Jimmy Carter explained the widespread looting that took place during the 1977 New York blackout this way:

> Obviously the number one contributing factor to crime of all kinds . . . is high unemployment among young people, particularly those who are black or Spanish-speaking or in a minority

age group where they have such a difficult time getting jobs in times of economic problems.

A month later, however, a New York study revealed that 45 percent of the arrested looters had jobs; only 10 percent were on welfare rolls. And consistent with similar case studies, the looters stole things for which they had no use or need.

Certainly poverty, racism, oppression, and substance abuse cannot be summarily dismissed as contributing factors to crime. Nor can they be tolerated in a society seeking to establish *shalom*. But they do not make people commit crimes. In fact, a recent study by University of Colorado sociologist Delbert Elliott found that race and class play only a minor role in crime among young people. After spending ten years studying seventeen hundred youths, Elliott concluded that poor blacks were only slightly more likely to commit crimes than their affluent white counterparts.

No matter what its aggravating causes, there is only one taproot of crime. It is not some sociological phenomenon; it is sin. Though men and women have essential dignity and value, we are predisposed toward evil choices. As Thomas Sowell writes: "People commit crimes because they are people—because they put their own interests or egos above the interests, feelings or lives of others."

This is the key to criminal behavior. We are sinners; we *choose* to do evil. A multitude of other factors influence what we do and become. But in the end we are responsible for what we do.

Saint Augustine in his *Confessions* gave what is perhaps the classic teaching on the nature of crime, reflecting Paul's argument in Romans 7:

> . . . I willed to commit theft, and I did so, not because I was driven to it by any need. . . . For I stole a thing of which I had plenty of my own and of much better quality. Nor did I wish to enjoy that thing which I desired to gain by theft, but rather to enjoy the actual theft and the sin of theft.
>
> In a garden nearby to our vineyard there was a pear tree. . . . Late one night a group of very bad youngsters set out to shake down and rob this tree. We took great loads of fruit from it, not for our own eating, but rather to throw to the pigs; even if we did eat a little of it, we did this to do what pleased us for the reason that it was forbidden.
>
> Foul was the evil, and I loved it.

Some scholars mock Augustine. Here, they say, was a philanderer and a heavy drinker. Surely he could think of more heinous sins than stealing a few pears from a neighbor's tree.

But they miss the point. The fruit, says Augustine, "was desirable in neither appearance nor in taste." We sin not primarily because of outside influences or factors beyond our control, but simply because we *choose* to sin.

Criminals break the law because they choose to do so. Their hearts, like Augustine's, are hardened. This is a Biblical and a theological doctrine. But it is also confirmed by the most credible social science analysis of criminal behavior.

In 1976 Dr. Stanton Samenow published *The Criminal Personality,* the result of seventeen years of clinical analysis by Samenow and his late partner Dr. Samuel Yochelson. The two researchers studied two hundred and fifty habitual criminals of various racial, economic, and environmental backgrounds, spending as much as eight thousand hours with some of them.

When Samenow and Yochelson began their research, they held the conventional view that criminals were merely the victims of social deprivation. What they found instead was that there is no easily definable social or economic cause of crime. In fact, they concluded that such explanations of crime serve only to buttress the criminal's view of himself as the "victim" of his family, his feelings, or his finances. Samenow wrote:

> We found with our people that they rejected the schools and their parents and responsible forces around them before ever being rejected by them. In other words, they were more victimizers than victims.

The Criminal Personality placed responsibility for criminal behavior squarely on the criminal himself. Criminals, not society, are the cause of crime.

Law professor James Q. Wilson has looked at the problem from a historical perspective. If crime were caused by societal conditions, crime rates should increase during times of social turbulence or economic need, and decrease in times of tranquillity and prosperity. But Wilson argues that history demonstrates otherwise.

In the middle of the nineteenth century, when rapid urbanization would lead one to expect increased crime, the level of crime actually fell. Why? Wilson argues that morality took hold just as industrialization began. It was during this period that a great spiritual awakening occurred.

Conversely, during the good economic years of the twenties crime began to rise. The reason, Wilson says, was that "the educated classes began to repudiate moral uplift, and Freud's psychological theories came into vogue." People no longer believed in restraining their children's sinful impulses; they wanted to develop their "naturally good" personalities.

Then came the Great Depression. Approximately thirty-four million men, women, and children—20 percent of the population—were without any income at all. Yet crime did not rise.

Wilson concludes that the key factor in crime rates is not external factors. It is individual character—the moral habits created by personal choice. Real reform can only take place, in Samenow's words, through "the deliberate conversion to a more responsible lifestyle." Or, as Norman Carlson, former director of the Federal Bureau of Prisons, puts it, "Change has got to come from the heart."

This is what motivates the work of Prison Fellowship and groups like it. We know that inmates are changed not by their confinement, but by choosing a new way of thinking and living—a new character. The means for that alternative is offered in the person of Jesus Christ.

This was illustrated in the experience of two public officials, then-Congressman, now Senator Dan Coats and Congressman Frank Wolf.

In 1985 Coats and Wolf traveled to California to visit a "model" juvenile facility, a youth detention center in Santa Ana, California, that was touted to be the best money could buy, the best modern minds could devise. It was an expensive, carefully designed program combining the latest psychology with the latest technology; hopes were high that it could nip young offenders in the bud and rehabilitate them.

Coats and Wolf were heartily depressed by their tour. Morale was low, the place could boast no improved recidivism rates, and the whole expensive program could be called a mediocre failure at best.

As their entourage prepared to leave, a young man named George, one of the teenaged inmates, stopped them. "You guys must be discouraged," he said.

They acknowledged they were frustrated.

"Well," he said, "I just want you to know that I'm gonna get out of here, and I'm gonna go back and finish high school, and I'm gonna go to college, and I'm gonna get married, and I'm gonna have children. *I'm* gonna make it."

Coats asked George why he was different, why he felt he could make it when so many others couldn't.

"A few months ago," the kid responded, "some volunteers from this organization called Prison Fellowship came and visited me. They told me about Jesus, and I became a Christian.

"And that's what's different about me. All the rest of the guys here just don't have any hope. *But I have hope.*"

The view that the criminal—not society—is morally responsibile for crime leads to an idea of justice very different from one based on the belief that crime is the response of good people to bad circumstances. Though modern sociologists and criminologists take offense at the idea of punishment, it is essential: If justice means getting one's due, then justice is denied when deserved punishment is not received.

Ultimately, lack of punishment undermines one's dignity as a moral, responsible human being. C. S. Lewis summed this up in his essay, "The Humanitarian Theory of Punishment":

> To be punished, however severely, because we have deserved it, because we "ought to have known better," is to be treated as a human person made in God's image.

Unfortunately, discredited theories of human perfectibility and the social origins of crime remain the foundation of our nation's criminal justice system. Criminals are victims rather than victimizers; societal evils, not sin, are the "fountainheads of crime."

Thus we are left with institutions—prisons—created in the mistaken belief that they can cure essentially good but misguided offenders. Now they simply warehouse more and more criminals in the decaying remains of this massive, expensive, failed experiment in rehabilitation and deterrence, a brontosaurus on the landscape of American life.

It is time for change.

Six

Restorative Justice:

A New Foundation
for Criminal Justice

We need criminal justice reform. We need reform because, simply put, the current system does not work. It ignores victims and their losses. Instead of rehabilitating offenders, it debilitates them. It wastes money. It is, on nearly every count, a dismal failure.

It fails because it attempts to do what no governmental system can do—change the human heart.

The failure is well-known. Why, then, are there not outraged demands for total overhaul of the criminal justice system? In a word, the reason is fear.

Most politicians fear nothing more than being branded "soft on crime." They view any innovation as a threat. So the status quo remains entrenched, and the public accepts the assurances of "experts" that the latest remedy (usually involving longer prison sentences) will clear things up.

But if there is to be real change, we must begin to ask some hard questions of those in charge.

■ Isn't there some way to make sure that victims are involved in the criminal justice process, without violating the rights of defendants?

■ Does it make sense that half of the people in prison are there for nonviolent offenses? Should prisons hold embezzlers, check forgers, petty thieves, and the like when cells are needed for rapists, murderers, armed robbers, and violent drug dealers?

■ Why should taxpayers be forced to pay exorbitant

amounts to keep nonviolent offenders sitting in prison cells that embitter them and make them more likely to repeat their offenses? Can't those offenders be made to work and pay back their victims and society?

With these questions in mind, we would like to propose a new approach to criminal justice, an approach that seeks to repair the wounds caused by crime as it seeks to prevent new crimes from being committed.

We call it Restorative Justice. It is being developed by Justice Fellowship, the criminal justice reform arm of Prison Fellowship, together with prison officials, legislators, theologians, and criminal justice experts around the country.

Three simple principles form the foundation of Restorative Justice:

- **First,** crime causes injuries that must be repaired.
- **Second,** all parties affected by crime should be included in the response to crime.
- **Third,** government and local communities must play cooperative and complementary roles.

Let's briefly look at each of these principles before outlining specific programs to accomplish them.

First, Crime Causes Injuries That Must Be Repaired
Victims, communities, and even offenders are hurt

by crime. The criminal justice process must address those injuries.

Victims such as Greg and Joan Browning sustain direct injury and loss. They should be compensated for those losses, given a voice in the court process, and assisted as they attempt to reestablish their sense of personal security. The criminal justice process should leave victims satisfied that their rights have been vindicated, not that they have been ignored or, even worse, made out to be the villains.

Communities are hurt by crime too. Crime can destroy public confidence in the community as a safe place to live. Unchecked, it can lead to disintegration of community values, even community dignity. It breeds fear and suspicion. Crime destroys *shalom*. Communities should be assured that the criminal justice process will help repair their losses and reduce the likelihood of future crimes.

Offenders injure not only their victims and communities, but their families and themselves as well. They should be held accountable for making amends for their crimes as well as given the opportunity to restructure their values and priorities.

Second, All Parties Should Be Included in the Criminal Justice Process

Not only government, but victims, offenders, and

communities should be actively involved in the criminal justice process, at the earliest point and to the maximum extent possible. The existing criminal justice system includes only the government and offender. The victim and community must also be included.

One way to begin is to grant victims a formal role in criminal cases in order to secure financial restitution. While this would be a complete departure from United States criminal justice practice, several western European countries allow victims to join civil claims for damages with criminal trials.

The trial of terrorist Mohammed Hammadi is a case in point. In 1988 Hammadi was on trial in West Germany for participating in the 1985 hijacking of a TWA flight, and for the murder of U.S. Navy diver Robert Stethem. Stethem's parents participated in the trial as co-plaintiffs with the government, represented by their own West German lawyer. Had this trial taken place in the U.S., the Stethems would have had no role at all.

The community must also become actively involved, particularly local churches. Perhaps the most essential element of any real change in the criminal justice system is the hope and transforming power Christians can offer to people touched by crime. This brings us to the third point.

Third, Government and Local Communities Must Play Cooperative and Complementary Roles

Government has the God-ordained responsibility to restrain evil and to preserve public order. It does so through its police forces, courts, and prisons. But communities also have a responsibility, and that is to create and preserve peace, *shalom*.

Government has the power and resources to arrest, prosecute, and sentence offenders. But reconciliation of victim and offender, and the reintegration of both into the community, can only be accomplished when the community becomes involved.

The Church brings unique resources to offenders that government programs cannot hope to effect. Christians, who are specifically called to care for the bruised and broken of society, can bring that hope. This means caring for offenders, both during and after their incarceration, as well as their families.

And Christians must bring this same love and compassion to those the offenders have harmed. The parable of the Good Samaritan is the story of a crime victim and the person who helped bind his wounds. Jesus said that the Samaritan had loved his neighbor. He told us to go and do likewise.

Would a criminal justice system built on these three principles really make a difference? We believe that it would. And we've seen that it has in some innovative programs across the country. If adopted, these reforms would lead to more stories like that of Betty and Arnold Blanchard.

The Blanchards were typical victims of crime. An elderly couple from a poorer section of Montgomery, Alabama, they made an easy target. (Most crime, in fact, is committed against the poor.)

One quiet evening, as the Blanchards watched television, a man with a stocking over his head slipped through a window screen in their back bedroom. The burglar found Arnold's wallet and took about $60. Alerted by a muffled noise, the Blanchards caught only a glimpse of the thief as he escaped the way he entered.

Sixty dollars was no small sum to the Blanchards, but it wasn't losing the money that was so disturbing. What bothered them most was the feeling that their home had been violated, that their sense of security had been so easily taken away.

The police, of course, had very little to go on. Only a tiny minority of such burglaries ever result in a criminal being arrested and convicted.

And under normal circumstances, this would have been the end of the matter. The Blanchards would have had neither their peace nor their property restored to them. They would have been left insecure and alone.

But six months later, Prison Fellowship area director Steve Longenecker conducted Alabama's first Community Service Project (CSP). CSPs take Christian inmates out of prison on furlough and put them to work repairing the homes of needy families in the community. Not only do the families benefit, but inmates are given the chance to pay their debt to society by helping others.

Steve secured support from many local churches for the CSP. Frazer Memorial United Methodist provided transportation for the inmates. St. Bede's Catholic Church supplied facilities for all the functions related to the CSP. And Joy Fellowship took care of reviewing potential recipient families.

When a representative of Joy Fellowship first approached them about participating, the Blanchards were a bit apprehensive about interacting with convicted offenders. But their house was in need of costly repairs, and they were reassured knowing that the furloughed prisoners were Christians. So they agreed to participate.

By the time the CSP was over, the inmates had insulated the attic, painted windows, exterior trim, and six rooms in the house, repaired plumbing in the bathroom and kitchen, replaced vinyl flooring in the bathroom, and replaced the outside door. The total value of their labor and the donated materials was about $8000.

The Blanchards had been victimized by a criminal. But the work—and the attitudes—of the inmates repairing their home also brought emotional healing to the Blanchards, who began to come to terms with their burglary. They began to feel and think differently about those in prison. During the project's second week, they invited one of the offenders to stay as a guest for dinner. And they later became Prison Fellowship volunteers.

The local community took an active part in the CSP as well. A black police officer hosted a white inmate, taking him out on patrol one night to show him what it was like to be on the other side of the law. A local circuit court judge led one of the weekday Bible studies. Several Christian ex-prisoners took part in the project to act as mentors for the participants.

At the end of the project, Alabama Commissioner of Corrections Morris Thigpen was so impressed that he challenged Prison Fellowship to conduct four CSPs a year in Alabama.

This type of project is, admittedly, a tiny light in the vast darkness. Crime is a problem that will touch everyone. Programs like this will only touch a few.

But if we are to find solutions to America's crime

crisis, they will need to include the elements found in Montgomery. Victims need to be cared for with personal compassion. Offenders need to be held accountable to repay their debt to their victims and to society at large. They also need to be offered the Good News of real rehabilitation—a conversion of priorities and values through Jesus Christ. And the Church and the community must be actively involved in the process of restitution, reconciliation, and restoration.

With these principles at work, working together, we *can* make a difference.

Seven

Programs That Work

We know the bad news: America faces a criminal justice crisis. Fortunately, there is good news too.

The encouraging news is that programs around the country demonstrate that Restorative Justice could help solve the crisis. A number of states and communities have begun to respond in new ways to victims' needs, and are exploring new sentencing options for the nonviolent offenders who now contribute to massive overcrowding in their prisons and jails.

These programs demonstrate that change is indeed possible, that criminal justice can restore. Some programs are based on new ideas; others are as old as the Scriptures. All hold promise if adopted on a broad scale.

Victim Assistance

Victims need help in dealing with what has happened to them. Sometimes they simply need someone to talk to as they try to sort out their anger, confusion, bitterness, and fear. Usually they need practical assistance, such as information about court proceedings, financial assistance, or referrals to construction companies who can repair damage to their home.

Whatever their need, most victims don't know where to turn for help. Yet growing numbers of excellent victim assistance programs are being developed. These include victim/witness assistance programs that help victims keep track of court proceedings or inform them about rape crisis hotlines and shelters for abused spouses.

Most programs are part of a governmental agency, such as the prosecutor's office or police department. Some are privately funded and operated. Very few are affiliated with a local church. Yet, as we've noted, this is an area in which Christians are both equipped and compelled by Scripture to lend a hand. More churches should venture into this exciting—and challenging—arena of ministry.

Restitution

We need to make sure that offenders repay their victims whenever possible.

One obvious benefit of this approach is that it takes care of the victim. Those hurt by crime deserve more than just the satisfaction of seeing their offender convicted. (Often they don't even get that satisfaction.)

But offenders benefit from assuming personal responsibility and performing purposeful work as well. Paying back someone they have wronged allows a criminal to understand and deal with the consequences of his actions. Psychologist Albert Eglash argues,

Restitution is something an inmate does, not something done for or to him. . . . Being reparative, restitution can alleviate guilt and anxiety, which can otherwise precipitate further offenses.

The Earn-It Program in Quincy, Massachusetts, is one of the best restitution programs in the country. It has successfully gotten offenders, even those who were initially unwilling or unemployed, to pay back their victims.

The unwilling have been gently but firmly convinced by a technique called "tourniquet sentencing," in which the alternative to paying restitution grows more onerous the longer he resists restitution. An offender refusing to pay will initially be sentenced to weekends in jail. If he continues to refuse, the sentence will be increased to a full week, then a month.

Most pay. The overall compliance rate is 70 percent for all offenders and 86 percent for juveniles.

Those who are unemployed are assigned to local businesses that have agreed to accept offenders to work at minimum wages. The business community has been very supportive of this program; some have even hired the offenders at the conclusion of their sentences. Thus the community, the victim, and the offender have all benefited from practical implementation of restitution principles.

Several states have established Restitution Centers—facilities in which nonviolent offenders live while they work at outside employment. Restitution is deducted from their wages.

Not only have these centers ensured that victims get paid back for losses, but they also save taxpayers money. In Georgia, for example, offenders paid more than $200,000 for restitution in fiscal year 1986. But the state also collected $1,293,000 for room and board costs, $905,000 in taxes, $680,000 in fines and court costs, and $539,000 for support of the offenders' families.

Community Service

As we have seen, the offender harms not only the victim, but the community as well. Performing free service is an excellent way for nonviolent offenders to pay this "debt to society."

While community service has been used at various times throughout history, it got its contemporary start in 1966, when California judges used it for indigent women who had violated traffic and parking laws. In 1973, the British government established a nationwide program that quickly grew to involve tens of thousands of offenders. Since then, this has expanded throughout the United States as well.

The District of Columbia, for example, has used community service sentences since 1977, with over one hundred and fifty agencies participating.

The Vera Institute in New York City operates a program for indigent repeat offenders. This highly-regarded program has a 90 percent success rate.

Although community service programs were developed to provide alternative punishments for poor offenders, there is no reason why they could not be expanded to include all nonviolent offenders, regardless of their economic status.

Community Corrections Acts

Thirteen states now have Community Corrections Acts (CCAs). These programs permit local governments to design, develop, and deliver sanctions such as restitution, community service, intensive supervision, and drug or alcohol treatment. Funding for the programs comes from the state, in return for the county's agreement to divert particular nonviolent offenders from prison. It's less expensive—and more beneficial for everyone involved—for states to fund local community corrections than it is for them to warehouse offenders in their prisons.

These acts ensure that offenders are put to work so they can make restitution to their victims. Justice Fellowship Task Forces have helped secure funding for these programs in Indiana and Virginia and have worked for passage of such programs in Arizona, Michigan, and Alabama.

Restitution is usually a key component of the program. In Kansas, for example, CCA offenders paid $361,302 in restitution in 1987. The programs can also provide for offender drug or alcohol treatment that would not be available in prison. Indiana counties have tailored programs that require completion of high school, job training, and substance abuse treatment. Properly managed, they are very safe for the community. Virginia's program has had a recidivism (repeat offender) rate of only 4 percent.

And CCAs conserve tax dollars. In Kansas the annual cost per offender is only $1500—compared with that state's nearly $11,000 per prisoner.

Intensive Supervision Programs

Intensive Supervision Programs (ISPs) allow probation officers to work with a small number of offenders. In some cities, probation caseloads are as high as three hundred per officer; under an ISP they are twenty to twenty-five offenders per officer.

As under most probation programs, offenders must work, go to school or look for work on a full-time basis, and abide by curfew requirements. Yet because these offenders have far more frequent contact with their officers, they are held far more accountable than they would be under overloaded officers. Georgia's program involves more than five visits per week. Florida's provides for daily unannounced visits.

Intensive supervision has proven to be effective in protecting the public. A federal study of Georgia's program found that the recidivism rate of intensive probationers was much lower than that of comparable prisoners, and that none of the new crimes were violent. While intensive supervision probationers did have a slightly higher recidivism rate than regular probationers, the study found that this was because they were more serious offenders than those placed on traditional probation. This was further evidence that the program was successfully diverting nondangerous offenders from prison.

As a result, intensive supervision is saving the state money. The report estimated that Georgia has saved $6,700 for each person diverted from prison into intensive supervision—a total of $13 million.

Victim-Offender Reconciliation Programs

Victim-Offender Reconciliation Programs (VORPs) allow victims and offenders who agree to the program to meet, in the presence of trained mediators, to discuss the crime and to work out a restitution agreement and other sentencing recommendations.

Victims benefit because they get repaid, but also because they finally have an opportunity to express anger, ask questions, and deal directly with the persons who injured them. Offenders begin to understand the consequences of their crime on the victim, and typically ask forgiveness.

Justice Fellowship helped establish a program (called VICTOR of the Midlands) in Columbia, South Carolina. Its first case shows the value of reconciliation. A farm produce distributor's business had suffered a rash of missing produce. After looking into the matter, he caught one of his employees stealing twenty-five bags of onions valued at $200. He fired the employee and pressed charges. The local judge referred the case to the VICTOR program.

During reconciliation, the offender offered to repay the value of the goods and to provide his ex-employer with information on how other produce was being stolen. Although the meeting was awkward (the ex-employee was ashamed, while the former boss was hurt and angry), the offender expressed remorse and apologized. The employer initiated a handshake at the end of the meeting—and all parties were pleased with the outcome of the case.

More than twenty states now have these programs, which handle both misdemeanor and felony cases. The program in Elkhart, Indiana, for example, handles felonies (typically burglary and theft cases) 60 percent of the time. The Genesee County Sheriff's Department in upstate New York runs an unusual victim-offender program which focuses on violent crimes such as assault, armed robbery, and negligent homicide.

In one year, Oklahoma's Post-Conviction Mediation Program handled one thousand meetings between victims and offenders, resulting in $300,000 in restitution agreements, $13,000 paid into a victim compensation fund, and thirty-two thousand hours of community service valued at $105,000.

These reconciliation programs are popular with victims. Seventy percent who were asked to participate in the Oklahoma program agreed, and 98 percent of them were pleased with the result.

Community Control
Florida established the Community Control Program in 1983. It is a statewide program of community service, restitution, and other sanctions enforced by what is in effect the nation's largest and most encompassing house arrest program. The state has mandated strict surveillance, requiring that Community Control officers have caseloads of no more than twenty offenders. Its current population is eight thousand offenders.

A recent study found that from 50 to 65 percent of Community Control offenders would otherwise have been sent to prison. Florida officials report that it has decreased prison commitments by one hundred and eighty per month, and that it has saved the state the equivalent of 7.5 prisons. The recidivism rate is only 27 percent, with only one-third for new crimes (the rest are for technical violations).

Will all this solve the criminal justice crisis? There are no instant solutions. But these approaches would go a long way in the right direction. Here's how they would affect the problems we discussed at the beginning of this book.

■ *Prison overcrowding*: Diversion of *nondangerous* offenders to work outside prison in order to repay their victims would reduce reliance on prisons. It would consequently ease prison overcrowding, freeing up space needed for the truly dangerous.

■ *Prison costs*: Community programs are far less expensive to operate than incarceration, and many generate revenue to support themselves. And they may reduce the need for new prison construction. It's time to save states from ever-expanding prison systems that don't rehabilitate offenders, don't repay victims, and cost taxpayers billions of dollars.

Of course, the costs of criminal justice in our country will continue to rise whether we take a Restorative Justice approach or not. Increasing our use of Restorative Justice programs will make most efficient use of scarce resources, especially when compared to the costs of ever-expanding prison systems.

■ *High crime*: Imprisonment increases the likelihood that property offenders will get into trouble again. If those offenders are sentenced to community punishments, repeat offender rates may finally begin to decline. Enforced restitution could help offenders learn about their victims and the dignity of work, and implement a change in priorities and lifestyle. Eased overcrowding increases the likelihood that violent and dangerous offenders will serve their full sentences.

■ *Forgotten victims*: No system can turn back the clock and cleanse crime's effects from victims. But Restorative Justice programs would give victims a significant role in the justice process, repayment by their offenders, and support from communities committed to doing justice.

So often politicians offer simple answers to complex problems—and the public is eager to accept them. The crisis in the American criminal justice system is serious. Tough talk won't solve it.

If we really want to get tough on crime, let's hold offenders accountable to their victims. Let's reserve prisons for hardened criminals (where they can be incarcerated for longer periods of time), and let's put nonviolent offenders to work. Let's give victims a meaningful say in the justice process, and let's put community resources to the task of binding the wounds caused by crime.

To really get tough on crime requires hearts sensitive to the demands of Biblical justice and righteousness. As we who are citizens lead the way, those in leadership cannot help but follow. There *are* real solutions to the crime crisis in America today. We've suggested some principles and ideas you can explore, in terms of what *you* can do, in your community, in the Appendix to this book.

The key to viable change and solutions to the crime crisis is for us all to work together in patience and perserverance—as the story which follows well demonstrates.

Epilogue

Doing Justice:

A Case Study

(Charles W. Colson)

Walla Walla, the Washington state penitentiary, has enjoyed a notorious reputation in America's prison system. When I first visited it in 1979, it was a simmering concrete caldron of rival inmate gangs, predatory homosexuals, demoralized guards, violent convicts, and frightened nonviolent offenders.

Four months before my visit a guard had been killed, and the prison had been locked down ever since, with inmates confined to their cells twenty-three hours a day. Anger and tension had mounted every day over those four months. The atmosphere seemed ripe for more violence. I arrived the very day after the lockdown ended; I could feel the tension in the air.

As I looked out over those who had gathered to hear me speak at a service in the prison's dingy auditorium, the small inmate audience looked back at me defiantly. Two particularly tough-looking prisoners sat in the front row, arms folded across their chests. As I began to speak, sharing the good news of the gospel and telling the inmates how Prison Fellowship was committed to caring for them, these men simply stared at me, their dark eyes unblinking. Even as I spoke, I found myself praying that somehow their hearts would be touched.

At the end they came to the front. Their expressions hadn't changed, but one extended his hand.

"I'm Don Dennis," he said quietly. "We've been talking, and we believe you."

Later I discovered what I was glad I hadn't known while I preached: a riot had been planned for that very afternoon. Six guards had been targeted for murder; there had even been talk of taking me hostage. But during my sermon God *had* touched their hearts; the inmate leaders had sensed sincerity and a real desire to help them. They called off the riot.

At that point it was clear that Walla Walla needed long-term commitment on our part. I commissioned George Soltau, Prison Fellowship's most experienced seminar instructor, to lead several Bible study seminars at the institution. George met privately with half a dozen inmates who were clearly ready to riot; they had long sentences, a lifetime of anger, no sign of hope ahead except the slender possibility that perhaps Prison Fellowship *could* begin to make a difference for them.

But George could tell that one misstep on our part and even this tenuous trust would be extinguished.

From the convict leaders George discovered that there had been no communication between inmates and the prison officials for a year and a half. He talked with Walla Walla's warden, who agreed to consider meeting with prisoner representatives.

That promise bought George some time. In the meantime several prisoners became Christians through the Bible study, along with Don Dennis, whose leadership in the prison now reflected his new walk with Christ. George and another Prison Fellowship staffer, Al Elliott, continued to visit Walla Walla regularly. Frustrations still ran high; some inmates attempted suicide as a protest against conditions, while others plotted more violence against guards. But the inmates held it in check—for by this time they had been told that the Washington state legislature had invited me to speak there about the situation.

Through the efforts of two public officials who are Christians, Robert Utter, then chief justice of the Washington state supreme court, and William ("Skeeter") Ellis, a state representative, I had the opportunity to address both the Republican and Democratic caucus committees, telling them in plain terms that Walla Walla was an explosive situation that needed to be diffused or it would wreak havoc for the state. The facts compelled the legislators to action; they passed a resolution vowing to deal with conditions at Walla Walla. It seemed like things were finally beginning to move.

Then Dan Van Ness, along with a Christian attorney in Seattle named Chi-Dooh ("Skip") Li, began to work with a committee of legislators and concerned politicians who were developing legislation that would address Walla Walla's specific problems. After his election Governor John Spellman appointed Amos Reed, a committed Christian as well as an able public official, to head the state corrections system. Amos immediately backed our reform efforts.

Then, in May 1980 the U.S. District Court ruled on a case filed by inmates complaining of conditions at Walla Walla. After hearing testimony regarding an inmate who had been sodomized by a guard, another whose leg had to be amputated after gangrene was neglected, another who was held naked in isolation for four days, and the startlingly blunt testimony of Warden James Spaulding, who said his prison ought to be "closed down," the court ruled that Walla Walla had violated the constitutional prohibition against "cruel and unusual punishment."

The inmates were jubilant. Hope for change in the institution finally seemed real. A court order transferred a number of inmates to other institutions to relieve Walla Walla's overcrowding.

But these efforts backfired, creating first overcrowding at the other prisons and then deadly riots. Angry, and exhausted, officials at Walla Walla tightened restrictions there—and the cycle of inmate violence and hopelessness began again. Warden Spaulding responded with another lockdown.

At this point I returned to Walla Walla and was permitted to visit inmates in the segregation unit. I found men who had been locked in dim, squalid cells for more than a year. Uneaten food and human waste lay on the cement floor outside the cells. It was like nothing I had ever seen before. The inmates' combination of rebellion and despair chilled my soul.

The odious situation deeply angered me as well. I emerged from segregation and confronted Warden Spaulding (who clearly was *not* willing to address the problem), and then the media (who were more than happy to do so). This led to a state investigation—and in turn, Warden Spaulding was transferred elsewhere in the system.

The incident added fuel to the fire building in the legislature, and among concerned citizens. The court appointed a liaison to work with the inmates; then, in the spring of 1981, the Washington state legislature passed the first in a series of real reforms. At our recommendation a sentencing commission established a policy to put nonviolent offenders in alternative programs. Early-release programs relieved overcrowding, and the state allocated funds to clean up and refurbish the prison. It seemed that there was hope at last for Walla Walla.

The years went by, and then came Easter morning, 1985. As we drove the long road approaching Walla Walla, it seemed like the same forbidding place that I had visited after its lockdown in 1979. But as we drew closer, it was clear this was a new Walla Walla.

The warden, Larry Kinchloe, enthusiastically met us at the gate and escorted us through the prison. In the protective custody wing—formerly a filthy, frightening place—the floors and walls were scrubbed clean, and most of the cells were freshly painted. Recreation areas had been added in every cellblock. The inmates seemed as different as the prison—relaxed, open, smiling.

At the chapel, the sense of renewal was complete. Bible studies and seminars at Walla Walla had been thriving for years now; as I spoke, this time there were no hostile faces and cold eyes, but warm grins, inmates carrying well-thumbed Bibles and cheering the reality of the risen Christ. For over the years between 1979 and 1985, they had seen the reality of His love lived out in people who cared for them—physically, spiritually, and emotionally—and then were willing to work hard on their behalf.

Granted, Walla Walla is still a prison facing tough problems. But in its fresh paint and new attitudes that Easter morning we saw a message of great hope: real change *is* possible. And it comes most often not through the efforts of any one or two individuals, but through a whole host of people working together.

Walla Walla went from riot to quiet through the

prayers and efforts of such people as Al Elliott and George Soltau, who worked patiently with the men, building relationships and trust when the conflict was at its height. Committed Christians in politics, including Justice Utter, Skeeter Ellis, and Skip Li, worked wisely and hard in sustained efforts to bring reform legislation before the people of Washington state. Inmates such as Don Dennis took leadership in the institution—and demonstrated the power of Christ to utterly transform lives. And prison officials such as Amos Reed showed that corrections officials can do much to bring about needed change in their institutions.

And the exciting thing is that even as I write, Washington state has one of the best prison systems in the country. Sentencing guidelines we helped to implement have worked. And significantly, the percentage of dangerous people now behind bars for *violent* crimes has gone up, while the percentage of nonviolent offenders in Washington's prison cells has gone down. This is how prisons should be used.

And while the rest of the country struggles with desperately overcrowded prisons, Washington's institutions actually have extra cell space. As a result, the state is leasing prison space to other jurisdictions.

In all, the story of this once-desolate prison shows us that, when watered faithfully, tiny seeds of hope can grow—even in the concrete jungle of a place like Walla Walla. When committed Christians faithfully fight the right battles in the criminal justice arena, God can use them to help restore broken lives and bring about real justice.

Appendix

What You Can Do

As the story of success from Walla Walla makes clear, real change comes about when people act out of hearts stirred with compassion for those touched by crime, and with righteous outrage and indignation over our wasteful, inefficient, often inhumane criminal justice system.

Successes in combating deep-seated social problems of the past follow this same trend. After all, such movements as the abolition of the slave trade and the great fight for civil rights began with grassroots activism. Effective change begins with you and me. You *can* make a difference in the crime crisis in America. Often ordinary people can be used in extraordinary ways. Here are just a few examples:

■ Al and Nadine Peters work a 500-acre farm near Hampton, Nebraska. For eleven years they have led a weekly Bible study at the Nebraska Center for Women in nearby York. Pictures of prisoners and ex-prisoners cover their kitchen bulletin board. They spend their vacations visiting women, now free, whom they first met in prison.

"We lost a son eighteen years ago," says Nadine. "Gregg's death prepared us to minister to the hurting. We can weep with those who weep and rejoice with those who rejoice."

■ Kent "Luke" Comegys was a loyal evangelical churchman and government official who never gave a thought to prisons. Inmates just didn't fit into his social circle. But at a friend's suggestion ten years ago, he began to visit a young black man named Everette Powell, who had just become a Christian in the Maryland Penitentiary in Baltimore.

Luke discipled Everette and watched as he discovered God's love. But Everette wasn't the only student; Luke discovered humility. God has shown Luke that he and Everette are equally important to their Creator, that eveyone is special in His eyes.

■ Myrtie Howell was ninety-one years old and confined to her home in Columbus, Georgia. But she wanted to reach out to men and women behind bars. She didn't allow her age or her physical condition to hinder her. Instead, she kept up correspondence with as many as seventeen inmates at a time and frequently sent Prison Fellowship what was obviously her "widow's mite."

■ Melissa Dorbeck, a Michigan homemaker and mother deeply committed to justice reform, serves as the special assistant to the Justice Fellowship Michigan Task Force. In addition to spreading the word about Restorative Justice in her community, Melissa met with legislators and public officials about the Community Corrections Act recently passed by the Michigan legislature.

■ In the early 1980s Florida's prison crisis was spiraling out of control. Between 1981 and 1982, the prison population had grown by more than forty-five hundred inmates. At this rate, the state would have been forced to build a new prison every two months to handle its new arrivals.

State spending for prisons had already risen 700 percent in ten years. The prison emergency threatened to swell the corrections budget by $100 million a year for the foreseeable future.

Legislators were reluctant to take bold action for fear that the public would not understand. What was needed was some clear public education.

So a group led by Florida businessman Jack Eckerd toured the state, meeting with legislators, religious leaders, business people, and media executives to spread the principles we've shared in this book: that prisons are expensive and should be used only for the most dangerous offenders; that Florida needed viable alternatives to incarceration such as restitution and community service for nonviolent offenders; and that sentencing guidelines were needed to make the most efficient use of prison resources.

The message caught on. Public response was enthusiastic. The media provided editorial support. And public officials found the courage to take bold, decisive action.

As a result, landmark prison reform legislation

passed the Florida legislature almost unanimously in 1983. A prison situation that seemed nearly hopeless began to turn around dramatically. The prison population dropped. In the first three years, the corrections budget increased by only $60 million instead of the projected $300 million. And what confounded conventional wisdom most was the fact that crime rates in Florida dropped as well.[1]

■ After being a victim of burglary himself, Lee Porter became chairman of the Justice Fellowship-sponsored Victim-Offender Reconciliation Program in Columbia, South Carolina. "We offer the victim a way to be meaningfully involved in the system," Lee says, "and to have an opportunity to receive restitution and healing of psychological harm done by crime."

■ Insurance agency manager Ross Osborne became a member of the Indiana Justice Fellowship Task Force because of his concern about the problems in the criminal justice system. He and other Task Force volunteers wrote letters, made speeches, and met with key state legislators and officials. They were instrumental in the legislature's providing a community corrections program and then giving needed funding for it. For Ross there is a lesson in this experience. "I've learned that a state is not too big a place to get changes made."

Like Ross Osborne, you can make a difference in your community. Here are some suggestions on how you can get started:

■ *Begin by becoming informed on criminal justice issues.* This book is just a start. It is vital that you find out what is happening in your state and local area. Advocacy must always begin with solid, current information. Are the prisons in your state overcrowded? Are there effective victim assistance and compensation programs in operation? Are nonviolent offenders usually sent to community-based sanctions?

There are several ways you can become informed. Read your newspaper carefully. Talk to local law enforcement officials and civic groups such as the Chamber of Commerce, which should be covering these issues. Contact your state representatives and ask them for information. Write or call Justice Fellowship for analysis of the situation in your state. (JF maintains fact sheets on each state that provide current information on key issues.)

If there are community service, restitution, or victim assistance programs in your city, call the director. You may want to ask for written materials describing what they do, or find out whether you can visit them.

Of course, the best way to become informed is to *get involved as a volunteer*. Prison Fellowship prepares and supports tens of thousands of volunteers across the nation and around the world to reach out to prisoners, ex-prisoners, and their families. Justice Fellowship works with people concerned about criminal justice issues.

At the time of this writing, Justice Fellowship is developing a pilot program to help church volunteers minister to crime victims. Although victim assistance programs exist across the country, very few are church-based, and most are incapable of responding to all the victims who would like help. We are convinced that ministry to victims should be a pressing priority for Christian ministry.

■ Another way to get involved is to *let other people know how you feel*. Write a letter to a public official. Because most people never write or call their elected officials, particularly on these issues, your representatives will pay attention to what you say. Write your local newspaper and radio and television stations. Many will print or broadcast your views, which will help influence other people in your community.

■ We would also encourage you to pray. *Pray for those touched by crime—victims and offenders—and those who work in the criminal justice system. And pray for public officials*. Scripture encourages us to pray for our leaders, and to pray for the peace and health of the place in which we live.

If you would like more information about Justice Fellowship, or would like to receive the *Justice Report*, a quarterly newsletter reporting on JF's news and views, please write to: Justice Fellowship, P.O. Box 17181, Washington, D.C., 20041-0181. If you would like to find out more about Prison Fellowship's ministry and would like to receive *Jubilee*, a monthly newsletter of Prison Fellowship, please write us at P.O. Box 17500, Washington, D.C., 20041-0500.

Notes

CHAPTER THREE

[1]New York later had to admit that its mandatory life sentence for drug dealers served as no deterrent: in spite of it, drug offenses continued to skyrocket, as did the prison population. The legislature had to repeal the law.

APPENDIX

[1]Criminal justice reforms are not static. Gains made one year may be lost the next. Florida's rising population, together with its growing drug problem, has led to rising crime rates—which produced a political outcry for more harsh sentences. And as we write, the state faces another prison overcrowding crisis. Justice Fellowship is again working with Jack Eckerd and other civic leaders to promote responsible reforms.